When Life Forces You to Pivot: A Reset Guide for Starting Again

By Tashia R. Jones

Published independently by Tashia R. Jones

ISBN: 9798995141815

First Edition

For more information, visit:
www.strongerthanb4.org

Dedication

For my children,

You taught me what it means to be present, to love fiercely, and to let go with grace. Watching you spread your wings was one of the hardest and most beautiful pivots of my life.

For every woman who has been told to move on before she's had time to grieve,

For the ones who wear the "strong friend" label like armor while crying in the shower,

For the mothers, whose houses have gone quiet,

For the professionals who gave everything to a company that saw them as expendable,

For the women rebuilding their lives at 40, 50, 60, and beyond,

This is for you.

You are not starting over.

You are starting from experience.
And you are stronger than before.

Table of Contents

Preface

I did not plan to write this book.

In fact, if you had asked me in 2024 what my life would look like a year later, I would have described something entirely different: stable, predictable, comfortable.

But life had other plans.

Last year, I became an empty nester. My son left for the military. My daughter got married. The house that once held noise, movement, and shared meals became quiet, so quiet it felt deafening. Around that same time, a long-term relationship ended. Nearly eight years of companionship dissolved, and with it, the future I thought I was building.

Then, just as I was trying to steady myself in the silence, I was laid off from my job.

At that moment, the job ending was the final shift. The last piece made it undeniable. This wasn't just a hard season. This was a reset.

I didn't choose it.

But I had to respond to it.

All of these changes forced me to pivot. And in that pivot, I had to decide who I was going to be and what this moment would mean. The small steps mattered. My mindset mattered. My support system mattered.

I struggled, questioned, and grieved what was. But I also leaned into faith. I read books that strengthened my thinking. I spoke affirmations aloud when my thoughts were heavy. I opened my Bible. I prayed. I had honest conversations with myself. I spoke life into places that felt like they were dying.

This book was born out of that space.

It is not just for women, although many women will see themselves here. It is for anyone who has experienced a forced pivot: an empty nest, a divorce, a long-term breakup, a job loss, a life change that pulled you out of your comfort zone without your permission.

This book is for the person who knows this cannot be the end, and for the one who needs to be reminded that you are enough.

You are allowed to take small steps. You are allowed to rebuild slowly. You are allowed to ask for help. You are allowed to grow in the middle of uncertainty. And you don't have to go through this alone.

My prayer is these pages encourage you not to suffer in silence. I hope they challenge you to see your pivot as a possibility and remind you who you are and "whose you are."
This is not the end of your story.
It is the beginning of your reset.

Tashia R. Jones

THE PIVOT

Chapter 1: When Everything Changes at Once

There are moments in life when everything changes, quietly or all at once, and no one asks if you're ready.

One day, you're following your usual routine and managing your responsibilities. Then, suddenly, something changes. Maybe a job ends, a relationship ends, or the house feels emptier. The future you thought you knew now seems strange or unfamiliar and people expect you to adjust quickly.

People say things like "Everything happens for a reason" or "You'll figure it out." They may not realize you're still in shock, just trying to breathe and understand who you are after everything has changed.

This book is for you if you're in that uncertain moment, when everything has shifted, and you're unsure what comes next.

Not the comeback yet.

Not the strategy phase.

Not the "I've got everything together" version of the story.

This is for the pause.

For the woman experiencing a pivot she didn't plan for, career shifts, relationship endings, new beginnings, becoming an empty nester, or all of it at once. For the one who feels grateful and grieving at the same time. For the one who looks fine outside but is recalibrating internally.

Life forcing you to pivot doesn't mean you failed.

It means something old has completed its chapter and that deserves acknowledgment before action.

Here, you don't have to hurry to find answers. You don't need to explain yourself. You don't have to downplay what this time has cost you or how it's changing you inside.

Don't approach this guide as a fix. Use it to steady yourself and reflect before moving forward.

Think of this as a way to find your balance again, accept what you've lost, and notice the strength that brought you here.

Remember, starting over doesn't mean you're starting from nothing, even if it sometimes feels that way. You carry wisdom, experience, faith, and resilience with you.

This is your reset point. You don't have to face it by yourself.

The Moment Things Shifted

Every pivot has a timestamp.

It's rarely a slow fade; it's usually a series of sharp, jagged breaks that leave you breathless.

Sometimes it is obvious, like a phone call, a conversation, or a notice you didn't expect. Other times, it can be quieter or scheduled. But it is a realization that something no longer fits. A feeling you can no longer ignore.

What makes it harder is that the world around you keeps moving. People continue their routines, and expectations remain.

Naming the moment things shifted is the first step in understanding why this season feels so heavy.

For me, the first break came in March 2025, when the noise in my house traveled across the country as my son left for the military. Then came May, when the man I had built a life with for almost eight years packed his bags after a really bad argument we both played a part in. By late August, exactly one week after my daughter's wedding, my relationship officially ended.

We had been together since February 2018 and engaged since July 2021. For a while, we looked perfect on paper, the tall, athletic couple everyone admired. But by May 2025, the foundation had cracked beyond repair. He moved out after one too many arguments where we both said things we couldn't take back.

We spent the summer in that painful limbo, not quite together, not quite apart. I kept hoping we'd find our way back, but deep down, I think we both knew it was over. On August 29, 2025, exactly one week after I watched my daughter say, "I do," he made the call that ended it for good. What had taken eight years to build disappeared in a single conversation.

I had planned to be a "Mrs." by now. Instead, I was sitting in an empty house, wondering how I'd gotten everything so wrong.

I thought I was managing it. I thought I was "strong." But the universe wasn't done with its reconstruction of my life.

Friday, October 31, 2025. 3:15 PM.

I remember the light in the room. I remember the weight of my own exhaustion. I logged onto a video call that lasted exactly ten minutes. I watched the woman on the other side of the screen. Her face was a mask of practiced sympathy. She didn't want to be there. She was looking at a woman who had given literal sweat, tears, and soul to a company, and she was telling me that, because of "staff reductions," my journey ended today.

In ten minutes, I lost my job, my health insurance, and my sense of direction.

When the screen went black, time didn't just slow down; it stopped. I sat there in the silence of a house that was already too quiet. I asked the air, "Was it me? Was I not enough?" She had assured me it wasn't personal or anything I did. **But when you've put someone else's brand on a pedestal while leaving your own dreams in the basement, it feels deeply, devastatingly personal.**

The anger hit first. Then the disbelief.

My mother, my sister, my friends, they all reached out. They tried to pull me back to the surface. **I felt like I was standing in a room with no windows, no lights, and no door. I was trapped in the dark.**

I opened my mouth to scream, to protest against the unfairness of a year that had stripped me of my son, my partner, and my livelihood in a matter of months.

But the cry that came out of me had no sound.

That silent cry is where the pivot begins. It's the moment you realize that the ground you were standing on wasn't as solid as you thought. It's the moment you realize that "before" is gone, and "after" hasn't been written yet.

If you are in that dark room right now, listen to me: The silence isn't the end. It's the space where your new voice is being formed.

Chapter 2: The Aftermath: Shock, Grief, and the Fog

Shock is a thief that doesn't take everything at once. It steals in layers.

People assume that because I am still standing, I am fine. They see me at committee meetings, volunteering at community events, smiling through conversations, and somewhere in their minds they check a box that says she is past the worst of it. Showing up looks like healing from the outside.

What they cannot see is the internal lag.

My body might be in the present, joining the planning call or helping coordination for an event, yet my nervous system is still somewhere else. It might still be sitting in that 3:15 PM video call where everything shifted. It might still be frozen in the moment the words landed and did not fully register. It might still be adjusting to rooms that feel larger than they used to, or routines that quietly disappeared.

Shock does not follow a schedule, and it does not always look dramatic. Sometimes it looks like this. People assume that because I am still standing, I am fine. They see me grocery shopping, answering emails, or showing up to church, and somewhere in their minds they check a box that says she is past the worst of it. Movement looks like recovery from the outside.

What they cannot see is the internal lag.

My body might be in the present, pushing a cart down aisle seven or responding to a text message, yet my nervous system is still somewhere else. It might still be sitting in that 3:15 PM video call where everything shifted. It might still be frozen in the moment the words landed and did not fully register. It might still be adjusting to rooms that feel larger than they used to, or routines that quietly disappeared.

Shock does not follow a schedule, and it does not always look dramatic. Sometimes it looks like this.

Numbness. I move through my day as if I am slightly outside of myself, watching my life through a window that needs to be wiped clean. Conversations happen around me. I respond at the right times. Later, I cannot remember what was said.

Brain fog. I stand in the grocery store under bright fluorescent lights, staring at rows of pasta longer than makes sense. The hum of the refrigerators feels louder than it should. My cart is still. My mind is crowded, yet I cannot make the simplest choice. I reach for one box, then put it back. I reread the label three times as if clarity might suddenly appear.

The "I'm fine" mask. I smile when someone asks me how I am. I say I'm good and adjust my tone, so it sounds steady. Meanwhile, my chest feels tight, like something invisible is pressing inward. My shoulders stay tense even after the conversation ends. I get into my car and sit there longer than necessary, staring at the steering wheel, exhaling a breath I did not realize I was holding.

Shock is not loud for me.

It is quiet and disorienting. It is the gap between what people see and what my body is still trying to process. I wake up tired after a full night's sleep. It is being surrounded by people and still feeling alone.

Grief does not wait its turn. It slips in beside the shock.

Some mornings I wake up and instinctively reach for routines that no longer exist. Some evenings I sit in rooms that echo differently. The air feels thicker. The quiet feels personal. I realize that while I am moving forward on paper, internally I am still catching up.

If you find yourself functioning on the outside while you are still shivering on the inside, you are not stuck. You are human. Adjustment takes time, especially when your life has sustained multiple hits in a single year. When you lose the Airman, the partner, and the paycheck in the span of a few months, your mind works overtime just to keep you breathing.

Do not let the world's timeline rush your recovery. The aftershock is real, and it is okay if you are not back to normal yet. Normal does not exist anymore. We are building something new.

Grieving What Ended, Even If It Was Necessary

Not all grief comes from a loss you wanted to avoid. Let that settle in your spirit.

Sometimes you grieve the very thing that needed to end. You can feel relief and sadness at the same time. Peace and pain can sit at the same table. That confusion is where many of us get lost. We think if we are relieved, we should not be crying. The truth is you are allowed to mourn the dream, even if the reality was draining you.

We are taught that grief is reserved for things we loved and lost. There is another kind of mourning that no one prepares you for. It is grieving the things that were quietly exhausting you.

Sometimes we stay in situations that look great on paper yet feel like slow poison in private.

In February 2024, I took what I believed was a leap of faith. I was the fifty sixth employee, handpicked by the CEO and a Senior Vice President who knew my work and wanted what I brought to the table. I left a stable consulting position because I thought I was stepping into something great. Within eighteen months, that greatness began to feel like a cage. The goalposts just did not move. They moved constantly. Expectations shifted weekly. My manager spoke with a tone that blurred the line between correction and disrespect.

To survive, I adjusted my anxiety medication. I paid a therapist to help me process my workweek. I lived in a state of triple checking, terrified of making a mistake. I worked long hours for recognition that felt smaller with each passing quarter. I traded my peace for a lifestyle and convinced myself the paycheck made the pressure worth it.

On the outside, my relationship looked like a magazine cover. We were a good-looking couple. Tall. Athletics. Attractive. The pictures were polished. The smiles were convincing. Inside the house, the air felt different. The floor was covered in eggshells. I perfected the art of shrinking myself. Many times, I took the blame just to keep the peace. I was not perfect. I could have shown up differently in certain moments. Resentment from old arguments-built walls around my heart. Still, I stayed. I had already lived through more than one divorce. I told myself, At your age, Tashia, this is as good as it gets.

I was loyal to a fault, even when the situation was not loyal to me.

When the layoff happened and the relationship ended, I felt crushed. As I sat in the quiet that followed, I realized I was not only grieving the loss. I was grieving the effort it took to hold up weights I was never meant to carry.

I will never forget the first Monday morning after the layoff. November 3, 2025. I woke up at six out of habit. Before giving God my first praise, I reached for my phone to check emails and messages. Then it hit me. I do not have to do this anymore. No urgent Slack notifications. No Monday morning dread. No manager speaking to me as if I had to prove my worth.

Relief should have come first. Instead, tears did.

I cried because I had spent eighteen months convincing myself that job was the place I would finally become Vice President of Delivery Operations. I had turned down other opportunities because I believed in the mission. I poured my genius into their vision while my own business collected dust.

Grief does not ask permission to make sense. You can mourn the effort. You can mourn the hope. You can mourn the version of yourself who believed it would work out, even when you now see it was unsustainable.

The same pattern showed up in my engagement.

I celebrated the start of 2026 in another country. December in Lagos, Nigeria, was beautiful. The air felt different. The energy felt lighter. I dreaded coming back to the States, yet I knew responsibilities were waiting. A job search. Bills. Reality.

About two weeks after returning, once my sleep schedule finally adjusted, I grabbed my jacket and a small velvet red pouch to run a necessary errand. I drove Stella, my SUV, about a mile and a half down the road and parked in front of a place I had passed countless times but never imagined entering.

Inside the pawn shop, the air smelled faintly metallic and stale. Glass cases reflected the harsh fluorescent lighting. I looked down at my bare ring finger while waiting for the manager to tell me how much eight years of loving someone would be worth in cash.

I felt light and heavy at the same time.

I was not missing him. I was missing the person I had tried to convince myself I wanted to be. I was mourning eight years of memories, both beautiful and painful. I was mourning the effort of trying to shrink myself into someone else's idea of love and absorbing blame to protect his ego.

He could be affectionate and distant within the same week. Silence became punishment. Touch became conditional. Affection depended on whether I stayed in line. If I played the role well, I received warmth. If I stepped out of it, he held onto grievances long past their expiration date. The emotional back and forth exhausted me.

He was my best friend. He was the person I wanted to tell you about my day. Truthfully, he knew more about me than I knew about him. Parts of him remained hidden, revealed only in moments of accident or argument.

As I scrolled through my phone deleting photos, my throat tightened. Grief rose up quietly, almost asking me to reconsider. Erasing almost eight years felt permanent. Still, I knew I could not carry those images into whatever was next. He had emotionally moved on long before I did. The disconnect was there long before the final conversation.

If you are crying over something you know you needed to leave, you are not confused. You are human. Allow yourself to grieve the dream, even if the reality was draining you.

I walked out of that pawn shop with $1,487 dollars in cash and no weight on my left hand. The ring was gone. My hand felt strangely exposed, lighter and heavier all at once. I sat in Stella's driver's seat for ten full minutes before starting the engine, just breathing, just existing. I did not know what came next. I knew I could not go backward. Sometimes that is the only clarity you need.

It is okay to cry for the job that stressed you out. It is okay to mourn the partner who made you feel small. You are not mourning the person or the position. You are mourning the hope you attached to them.

The forced pivot was a rescue mission. Life recognized what I would not release on my own, so it closed the doors for me.

If you feel a strange mix of deep sadness and sudden lightness, do not question it. That is often what freedom feels like.

You are allowed to miss the perfect picture while being profoundly relieved that you no longer have to live inside the frame.

Chapter 3: When You Don't Recognize Yourself Anymore

Our identity largely comes from what we do and who we're connected to. When those things change, you don't just lose a role; you lose your "Who."

Don't move too fast. This pivot season isn't about becoming someone new overnight. It's about listening to who you already are, beneath the noise of everyone else's expectations. For a long time, my "Who" was tied to the Airman, the Bride, and the Delivery Leader. I was the woman planning a wedding, preparing to finally be a "Mrs." for the long haul.

But by November 2025, those titles felt like clothes that no longer fit.

When my son left for the Air Force, I lost my "daily mom" rhythm. When my engagement ended, I lost the future I had already started decorating. And when that video call ended, I lost the title that had been my armor.

I felt discarded because I had built my identity on rented land. I had poured my genius into someone else's empire while my own brand, Stronger Than Before Creative Services, which I've owned since 2008, sat on the back burner. I had let a W2 convince me that my own calling couldn't sustain me.

The identity crisis didn't announce itself with a bang. It crept in through the small, daily moments that used to define me.

When both my kids were in high school, I started noticing the shift. They got part-time jobs, made plans with friends, and became more independent. Dinner stayed on the stove longer, or I'd text them: "Your plate is in the microwave." My partner worked long hours, so most nights I sat at the table alone or in front of the TV watching something on Netflix. These were small, tiny pivots I didn't pay attention to at the time.

When my son was in eighth grade and my daughter in eleventh, it hit me for the first time: They didn't need me the way they used to. I tried to insert myself in places I could without being overbearing, but I was grasping at a role that was naturally evolving.

My mother, being the professional counselor that she is, posed a question one day: "Who are you without the mom title?"

I paused. I searched for an answer that wasn't textbook or cliché. I came up empty.

I didn't know who I was outside of being a mom and caregiver. That realization stung, especially when my partner would complain that I didn't pay him enough attention. He didn't have biological children of his own, so it was hard for him to understand the burdens and blessing mothers carry, the way we put our children above our own needs and often above our significant others.

I tried to reassure him: "Once the kids leave the house, it'll be just me and you. A different kind of life. We'll find our way back to that hopeful feeling we had when we first started dating." I was looking forward to it. I really was.

But that time came too late.

With both children spreading their wings, I was left trying to figure out meals just for me. I wasted so much food because I'd always cooked for three, four, sometimes five people. There was no one to wake up anymore. No doors to knock on and say, "Good morning, son. Good morning, daughter."

The small rituals that used to anchor my days disappeared one by one.

No more rollover good mornings in the hallway. No more knocking on bedroom doors to make sure they were awake. No more tea or coffee made each morning, tailored to their preferences. No more breakfast sandwiches or omelets they loved.

I worked from home, and giving those daily hugs and kisses goodbye, those tight embraces where you feel the faint beating of another human's heartbeat, were gone.

I miss hugs and physical confirmation that I matter to someone in a tangible, everyday way.

When my daughter comes to visit now, I look forward to the

moment the door opens and she says, "Hey, Mommy," and gives me the biggest, tightest squeeze that lifts me off the ground. Even at 24 years old, married and building her own life, I still see that adorable five-year-old smile that lights up my world.

She only lives a few cities over, but those 30 minutes feel like hours. College took her away first, then love. I missed our daily talks, our walks, and watching our shows together. I'm grateful we still steal a few lunch dates or wine, and chill moments a couple of times a month.

The professional identity crisis hit just as hard.

November 3, 2025. I woke up, did my morning routine, walked downstairs to my office, sat at my desk with two monitors and two laptops. I opened my work laptop and thought: Wait. This isn't a dream. I really don't have a job anymore.

Just weeks earlier, I had been praised and spotlighted for rolling out a yearlong operational delivery process that would streamline team efforts across the enterprise. I had influence and a title that opened doors.

Now, I had nothing but a laptop I needed to pack up and ship back.

I started removing my personal files, transferring them to my personal drive. Each file I transferred like the project proposal templates I spent months perfecting or the financial analysis report templates I poured over late at night felt like I was carefully boxing up a memory or achievement that represented my growth and dedication during my time at the company. With every click, I wasn't just moving digital documents; I was letting go of small pieces of my identity shaped by those challenges and successes.

I had given this company my best hours, my brightest ideas, my loyalty, and they removed me like a line item in a budget cut.

When people asked, "What do you do?" In those first weeks, I avoided the answer entirely.

I tried to cling to the identity I had forged through hours of dedication. A part of me was exhausted, but part of me was also riding a strange high. One week before the layoff, Saturday, October 26, 2025, I had been celebrated and crowned Ms. Alumni 1st Runner Up during Homecoming weekend at my alma mater, NCCU.

The last six months of my life involved months of campaigning, working 50 plus hours a week, planning and executing my daughter's wedding, being a supportive military mom, active in my sorority and alumni chapter, ending one relationship, establishing a new relationship, and being elected VP of the local alumni chapter. I was doing it all and I was hiding in plain sight, slowly unraveling.

I thought I'd bounce back quickly. I rolled up my sleeves and told myself: *Look at your resume. Look at your experience. You'll find a job in no time.*

I had only been unemployed once before. The banking crisis that shook the nation in 2007 collided with my personal life unraveling. By September 2008, I was divorcing my son's father, and everything felt uncertain at once. That season pushed me into one of the most pivotal journeys of my life, a journey that would take across the country and years to stabilize.

In 2010, life redirected me from Southern California back to North Carolina. Even in the middle of that disruption, I found work quickly. A friend from church told me about a contract opportunity at his company. I stepped into it without fully realizing that it would change everything. That contract role became the doorway into Information Technology and reshaped my professional path.

But this time, a month after being laid off, with unemployment benefits ending in two months, I still hadn't secured full-time employment.

I changed my LinkedIn profile four, maybe five times. Each version felt like I was trying on different versions of myself, none of them fitting quite right. I looked at my business cards from the old job and felt like I was staring at a stranger.

The only solace I had was that my planned December trip to Africa, a trip to explore the motherland and meet my new partner in person, was going to be a real vacation. One my spirit and soul desperately needed.

But before I could get there, I had to survive the daily silence that filled my home.

When the titles fell away and I no longer recognized myself, I thought I had lost something permanent. What I did not realize then was that the unraveling was not erasing me, it was revealing me.

When the roles that once held you together begin to loosen, it does not always mean you are lost. Sometimes it means you are finally shedding what no longer fits and meeting the person who has been underneath it all along.

Chapter 4: The Silence That Speaks

It was Saturday, September 3, 2025. A beautiful, sunny morning. I was dressed and ready for what was supposed to be a fun-filled day. I hurried out the back door to make my way down the road to my alma mater to volunteer at a home football game.

I loaded two dog beds, toys, food, and an overnight bag into the car. I shuffled my two dogs into the back seat, Taj, a twelve-pound hyperactive Maltipoo, and Josephine, Jojo for short, a seventy-pound, extra-nervous but super sweet American Pit Bull Terrier. I slid into my black Cadillac XT5 SUV, the one I affectionately called Ebony, and pulled out of the garage.

As I drove to drop them off at their respective babysitters, Taj kept trying to climb into the front seat to get to me. I kept reaching back, trying to calm him down. "Why didn't I put you two in the far back?" I muttered to myself.

I turned my head for a split second to settle them.

The next thing I remember was a man standing outside my car, his lips moving. I could not hear him, but I could read the words.

"Are you okay, ma'am? I'm going to pop the airbag and get you out."

I nodded.

Then I realized I had driven my pretty Ebony straight into a utility pole, splitting it in half and totaling my car.

Sometimes the hardest part of a pivot is not the noise of the crash. It is the silence that follows.

A quieter home, a lighter schedule, or fewer demands should feel like relief. Instead, they feel like a vacuum. You notice it in small, agonizing moments. You sit with your phone inches away, waiting for it to light up, hoping for a text, a call, an invitation, anything that reminds you that you are still connected to the world.

To drown it out, you perform. You scroll mindlessly through social media until your eyes ache. You binge watch show after show, not because you care about the storyline, but because fictional noise feels easier than your own thoughts. You might even talk yourself into an RSVP, only to send your regrets at the last minute because you cannot bear the thought of anyone seeing what is really happening behind your mask.

Silence becomes an enemy because it makes your thoughts louder. Old worries resurface. New questions form. You begin questioning your body, your faith, and whether you are exactly where you are supposed to be. There are moments when you pray without words, sitting in stillness, hoping that what feels uncertain right now is still being held by something higher than you can see.

For me, that October layoff turned my house into a battlefield of stillness. It felt too large. Too empty. The relationship had already ended months earlier, and by May the house had shifted into a different kind of quiet. My son was gone. My daughter was building her own life. The everyday movement that once filled the rooms had faded. There was no laptop glowing with urgent demands from a company that replaced me in a weekend. No calendar packed with meetings. No noise to distract me from myself.

I retreated into the dark. I felt as if I were in a room with no lights, no door, and no way out.

In early August, during the scholarship campaign, I met a Nigerian entertainer on a TikTok livestream. He had magnetic energy, the kind that filled the screen without trying. At the time, it was just work. His company, MDE Empire Promotions, helped amplify the campaign online, and we connected over the project. He was professional, kind, and lived halfway across the world.

We started talking more in early September. It was casual at first, just conversations that stretched longer than expected. By late September, as I was finally accepting that my eight-year relationship was truly over, those conversations began to feel intentional. It was not planned. It was not a rebound. It was simply two people connecting while I was still clearing the debris of what had ended.

In the aftermath of the layoff, as I sat in that dark room with no windows, he checked in. Not with clichés or motivational quotes, but with presence. He did not try to fix me or rush me. He just listened. He saw me.

And in a season where I felt invisible to a company, to a role, and even to myself, being seen mattered.

The six-hour time difference meant I stayed up later than I should have, but for the first time in years, I was not performing. I was not making myself small. I was not taking the blame to keep the peace.

I was just Tashia.

But still, the silence was deafening.

In that quiet, the thoughts I had been outrunning for eighteen months finally caught up to me. I thought back to May 2001, walking across the NCCU stage with my daughter in my belly. I was a warrior then. I had survived so much. So why did I feel so powerless now?

I realized the silence was loud because it was forcing me to listen to my own heartbeat. For years, I had used the noise of Delivery Leading and everyday motherhood to avoid a terrifying question: Who am I when I stop doing for everyone else?

In that dark room, I let out a cry that had no sound. It was a cry of anger for putting someone else's company ahead of my own brand. A cry of grief for the "Mrs." I would not become. But in that soundless cry, I felt something shift.

The silence was not there to swallow me. It was there to clear the room.

The house was quiet so I could finally hear the name of my own business whispering back at me: Stronger Than Before. I had owned that name since 2008. I built the business in 2018. But in 2025, I was finally being invited to live it.

If your home feels like an enemy right now and you find yourself avoiding the world, do not beat yourself up. **You are not lacking. Your heart is simply catching up to your new reality.**

This is recalibration.

The silence is loud because the previous version of you is leaving.

Let it go.

Something better is trying to speak.

Reflection & Pause

Take a moment before going ahead. This isn't about fixing problems or making plans but simply becoming aware of your current state.

There's no need to answer these questions perfectly or quickly. Just being aware is enough for now.

Reflection:

1. What has ended in this season of your life, even if it needed to end?

2. What emotions have surprised you during this pivot season?

3. In what ways has this pivot affected how you see yourself?

4. What feels heavy right now?

5. What feels hopeful, even if you cannot explain why yet?

Dig Deeper (Optional Journaling):

1. **Identity Inventory:** List the roles you've held in the past year (mother, employee, partner, friend, daughter, etc.). Circle the ones that have shifted or ended. How does it feel to see them written out?

2. **The Daily Rituals:** What small daily actions used to define your day that are now gone? (Making someone's coffee, sending a good morning text, logging into a work system, etc.) Which one do you miss most?

3. **The Question You Avoid:** When someone asks, "What do you do?" or "How are you doing?" what do you want to say vs. what you actually say?

4. **Future Self Letter:** Write a letter to yourself one year from today. What do you hope to tell her about this season?

5. **Permission Slip:** If you could give yourself permission to feel one "unacceptable" emotion without judgment (anger, relief, jealousy, fear), what would it be? Why?

THE PAUSE

Chapter 5: Permission to Rest

After a pivot, there can be pressure to keep moving. It's okay not to be okay.

The outside world expects you to stay productive, positive, and to prove that you are fine. We all do an excellent job of masking what is really going on and suffering in silence.

You may feel the urge to push yourself forward before you have had a chance to steady your footing or heal from heartbreak. We fill the quietness with action and show strength by staying busy.

I will tell you, from experience, that constant movement is not always progress.

For most of my life, I believed that if I wasn't moving, I wasn't mattering.

I spent the majority of my adult life defining myself by how present I could be. There was a reason for that. As a teenager, I gave birth to a child, but my family decided it was best for him to be raised by my aunt and uncle. That decision shaped me. So, when I had my daughter in 2002 at twenty-three, and my son in 2005, I didn't just want to be a mother; I wanted to be THE mother.

I was dedicated to being present for every major and minor life event. I worked, went to graduate school, and served in the church, but I still made sure I was the track coach, the cheerleading coach, the PTSA president, and the science project manager. I baked the cookies. I drove the carpools. I was determined to prove that I could do it all.

I kept that pace through elementary school, middle school, and high school. I was a machine of maternal devotion.

Then came the crash of 2025.

After the layoff and the breakup, my instinct was to do what I had always done: Push harder. I wanted to fill the silence with noise. I wanted to say "Yes" to everything because "No" felt like failure.

But I will tell you from experience: Constant movement is not always progress. Sometimes, it is just trauma in a tuxedo.

The silence of the empty nest wasn't just about my kids leaving; it was about the audience leaving. I had been performing "Super Mom" for two decades to prove I was worthy. When the house got quiet, I didn't know who I was without the applause, the busy schedule, or the chaos.

Sometimes what you need most is permission to stop pushing. You have nothing left to prove. You have raised the children. You have baked the cookies. You have led the meetings. It is time to sit down.

Chapter 6: When Your Body Keeps the Score

We often think mental health struggles happen all at once, but usually, they are a slow accumulation of debt.

My debt started piling up in March 2020.

When the world shut down, I was comfortable in my career, working a hybrid schedule. But suddenly, my home became a pressure cooker. I had a high school senior missing her milestones and a freshman son threatening to disappear behind a computer screen. I had a partner working outside the home, exposing us to a virus that terrified me.

I didn't pause then. I pushed. I tried to manufacture "normalcy" for my daughter's senior year. I tried to be an emotional anchor for my partner. I carried the weight of the world's panic inside my own chest.

When the world opened back up in the fall of 2021, I didn't exhale. I just ran faster. My daughter went to college, my son went back to school, and I threw myself into wedding planning and career climbing. I kept busy year after year, ignoring the check engine light on my soul.

By 2025, the bill came due.

I had pushed so hard to avoid the quiet that I didn't realize I was breaking. I gained weight, and with every pound, I lost a piece of confidence. I felt heavy, physically, and spiritually. When I glanced at my reflection, I barely recognized the woman looking back at me.

Mental health in a pivot isn't just about "feeling sad." It's about the exhaustion of holding it together for five years straight. It's the realization that you have been surviving, not living.

If you are feeling disconnected, heavy, or anxious, do not judge yourself. You are paying off the debt of stress you accumulated while you were being strong for everyone else.

But debt isn't just emotional. It's physical. And by the time I realized that my body was already keeping the score.

When Your Body Performs Instead of Rests

When you ignore your spirit, your body doesn't just scream; sometimes, it performs.

For decades, I treated my body like a rental car, driving it hard, ignoring the check engine light, and assuming it would just keep running. By the time my son left for the Air Force on March 18, 2025, my tank was completely empty. But instead of stopping to refuel, I redirected.

Between March and October, I threw myself into a scholarship fundraising campaign for NCCU. I poured every ounce of my "Delivery Leader" energy into it, raising over $20,000 for deserving students. I was feeding other people's dreams while mine were still in the dark.

I also started working out every single day.

With my long-term partner moving out, I was fueled by a complicated cocktail of spite and self-preservation. A part of me wanted to look good so he could see exactly what he was missing, even though I knew deep down I didn't want to stay. I was eating less. I was pushing more.

On the surface, it looked like a victory. People saw the weight loss and the "snap back," and they cheered. But the eyes behind the silhouette told a different story.

I was sleeping less and vibrating with frantic energy. My body was shedding weight not because I was healthy, but because I was in a chronic state of emergency. I was cannibalizing my own reserves to keep the lights on for everyone else.

Your nervous system needs safety, not just a smaller size.

Here's the uncomfortable truth I had to face I was using my body as a revenge plot instead of a healing tool.

Every workout was a message to my ex: Look what you're missing. Every pound lost was evidence that I was "winning" the breakup. But my body wasn't celebrating, it was in survival mode. I wasn't nourishing it; I was punishing it for not being enough to keep him.

That realization hit me hard one morning when I caught my reflection. Outside, I looked good. People were complimenting the weight loss, the "glow up," the way I had "bounced back." But my eyes told a different story. They were hollow. Tired. Desperate.

I was performing "wellness," not experiencing it.

If you're in that space right now, if you're exercising out of spite, restricting out of anger, or using your body to send a message to someone who's no longer watching, please hear me: Your body is not a billboard for your healing. It's the home you have to live in long after they're gone.

Stop weaponizing your temple. Start honoring it.

Safety looks like recognizing that "looking good" is not the same as "being well." You are allowed to stop the performance. You are allowed to let your body rest, to feed it without guilt, to move it with joy instead of rage.

Your body carried you through the breakup. It deserves your kindness, not your punishment.

Chapter 7: Faith When the Weight Is Too Heavy

There is a heavy cost to being a "Strong Friend."

You know who I'm talking about. The one everyone calls for advice. The one who organizes the trips. The one people rarely check on because "she always has it together."

I wore that label like a badge of honor, but in 2025, it felt like a noose. I was exhausted and mentally drained. But because I had spent twenty years being the coach, the president, the leader, and the rock, I didn't know how to take the cape off. I didn't know how to tell people, "I am not okay."

Faith during a pivot is tricky when you are the strong one. You feel like you're supposed to have a testimony, not a test. You feel like your prayers should be full of power, not desperation.

But God doesn't need your performance; He needs your presence.

Praying was hard for me during this season.

A part of me was confused about why I was going through another storm. I thought I was doing what I was supposed to do on the job and as a mom. But honestly? I was doing the basics with God too.

I'd wake up at 5:30 AM daily and whisper, "Thank you for waking me up this morning." Then I'd open my phone, go to the Bible app, do my daily devotional, and say a short prayer. I had over 800 consecutive days logged in the app. I loved seeing the badges, and the streak record. It was almost like a game.

But I was giving God the least of me instead of the best of me.

Maybe God was teaching me a lesson. This wasn't the first pivotal moment that changed the course of my life. Being molested from ages four to eight. Sexually assaulted at twelve. Preyed on by an older man at fourteen. Having a child at fifteen. A first marriage filled with infidelity. Later relationships filled with physical and emotional abuse.

I've had pivoted moments my whole life where I had to be strong, stronger than I care to admit.

Before the pivot, my prayers were full of declarations. I spoke with authority. I claimed victories. I stood on scripture like it was a weapon against the enemy. My faith was loud, public, and performative in the best sense. I wanted people to see God working in my life.

But in that empty house, after the layoff, after the breakup, after my son left for basic training? I couldn't find that voice anymore.

My prayers became whispers. Sometimes they were just tears. I'd sit on the edge of my bed with my Bible app open, and I couldn't even find words to ask for what I needed. I just needed Him to see me.

There was a moment in early November when I was scrolling through old voice notes on my phone. I found a recording of myself from 2022, praying aloud for my family, my business, my future wedding. That woman sounded so sure. So strong. So full of faith.

And I realized: I couldn't be her anymore. I had to let her go.

That's when I found Psalm 34:18: "The Lord is close to the brokenhearted and saves those who are crushed in spirit."

Not close to the ones who have it together. Close to the broken.

That scripture became my permission slip to stop performing faith and start experiencing it. I didn't need to move mountains right now. I just needed to believe He was in the room with me, even when it felt dark and still.

The song "I'll Say Yes, Lord" was on my lips daily throughout those times when I found it hard to cope.

As a survivor of an attempted suicide years ago, I had promised myself I would never leave my kids with that hopeless legacy. So, when the lyrics say, "Where You lead me, I will go, I will say Yes, Yes, Yes," that was all I could say.

My life was not my own, and my faith had to carry me through. I didn't have a choice.

The weight of the world sat heavy on my shoulders, but I had a Father who whispered to me, "Give me your burdens." It was hard to let go. I'm still learning to lean on God instead of carrying everything myself.

Did I struggle with feeling like God was silent or distant?

Yes, and sometimes I still do.

But I've learned there's a difference between silence and distance. I feel like God is silent at times, not answering my prayers in my timing, not moving the way I think He should move. But He's not distant.

I know God is right there, ordering my steps, inside the trenches with me, guiding me and keeping me in perfect peace when literally nothing around me is firm.

It feels like I'm in the middle of the ocean, tasting the salt, waves hitting me, the shoreline nowhere in sight. But God is still my life raft and my jacket, confirming He's with me even when I can't hear His voice.

What did it look like to "let God manage my tiredness"?

Honestly? I'm still learning.

My soul has been tired for a while. I don't know how to fully let God carry it, so I just cry out to Him: "Lord, You promised me You wouldn't give me more than I can bear, and I am at my limit!"

I found myself yelling that when I felt suffocated by financial pressures, the pressure to perform, the pressure to look like everything was okay. I was stapling my mask to my face so no one could see the pain of my tiredness.

There were moments in that empty house when I couldn't find the words. I was waiting to hear from my son at basic training, praying he was safe. I was waiting for a text from my now married daughter. I was adjusting to living alone for the first time in forever.

My faith had to shift from "Moving Mountains" to "Mustard Seeds."

I had to learn that it's okay to be weak. It's okay to lay down the burden of being the Strong Friend, the Super Mom, the Perfect Employee. God can manage your tiredness. He can manage your questions. You don't have to carry the world today.

When I confessed to my friend that I felt overwhelmed and needed support, I discovered how liberating it could be to release my need to seem strong. During that honest moment, I was reminded that God would help me manage both my fatigue and my uncertainties.

To everyone who feels the pressure to be everything for everyone else whether you're a parent, a devoted friend, or someone striving to be the perfect employee or partner, this is for you. It's okay to lay down the burden of being the Strong Friend, the Super Mom, the

Perfect Employee. You don't have to carry the world.

Chapter 8: Releasing the Timelines That No Longer Serve You

The hardest shift for a parent is moving from "Everyday Manager" to "Wise Counsel."

When my son left in March 2025, the routine I had lived in since 2002 disappeared in an instant. I wanted to reach for something that had always been there and suddenly finding empty space. The sadness was heavy, and anxiety crept in as I realized how much I depended on his presence. Some mornings, I woke up feeling hollow, unsure if I wanted to start the day at all. The house seemed quieter than ever; even the ticking of the hallway clock felt louder in the emptiness. I missed hearing his laughter as he played games, and the distant sound of his voice on Discord chatting with friends—a backdrop I never realized meant so much until it was gone. I didn't know what to do with my hands or my time, and the silence magnified every ache of loneliness.

I felt like I was running out of time. I'm in my 40s, I thought I shouldn't be starting over. I shouldn't be single. I shouldn't be unemployed.

But timelines are just imaginary prisons we build for ourselves.

Even as I was letting go of the old, a new energy was trying to reach me. Across the world, I met someone who began to awaken pieces of me that had been dormant for years. For the first time, I felt seen for me, not just for what I could "deliver."

Yet, even in that beautiful new connection, I struggled to release the timeline of "perfection." Because of the six-hour time difference, I stayed awake when my body was begging for sleep. I was determined not to repeat the mistakes of my previous eight-year relationship. I was going to be the "Perfect Partner" even if it meant sacrificing the very "Pause" I was writing about.

I was a highly functioning ghost, raising thousands of dollars for students, keeping a "revenge body," and navigating a new love across continents, all while my own foundation was still shaking.

Releasing the timeline means accepting that you cannot build a new life on the ruins of an old one if you haven't stopped to clear the debris. It means realizing that the "Super Mom" era has retired and the "Wisdom" era has begun.

You are not late. You are not behind. You are exactly where you need to be to learn that your value isn't tied to how much you can do on three hours of sleep. The "Pause" isn't a delay; it's the preparation.

Reflection Before Rebuilding

Before rebuilding anything new, it helps to take inventory of where you are.

This is not a moment to fix or decide. This is a moment to notice what your body, mind, and spirit have been carrying.

No judging. No rushing. Just reflecting. You do not need clarity or a plan right now. This pause is part of the process. Work the process.

Reflection:

1. Where have you been pushing yourself when you needed permission to rest?

2. What thoughts or emotions have been hardest to sit with in
   this season?

3. What has your body been asking for lately?

4. Where do you feel pressure from timelines that no longer serve you?

5. What helps you feel calm, safe, or grounded, even briefly?

Dig Deeper (Optional Journaling):

1. **Body Scan:** Close your eyes and do a mental scan from your head to your toes. Where are you holding tension? What does your body need that you've been ignoring? (Sleep? Movement? Stillness? Touch?)

2. **The "Super" Roles:** What role have you been performing that's exhausting you? (Super Mom, Strong Friend, Delivery Leader, Perfect Partner?) What would it feel like to retire that role, even temporarily?

3. **Faith Check In:** How has your relationship with God, faith, or spirituality shifted during this season? Are you angry? Confused? Distant? Clinging tighter? Write Him a letter with no filter.

4. **Timeline Rebellion:** What timeline are you holding to that's making you feel "behind"? (Age, career milestones, relationship status, financial goals?) What would happen if you released it?

5. **Micro Moments of Peace:** List 3 to 5 things that made you feel calm or grounded in the past week, even for 30 seconds. (A song, a hug, a sunrise, a text from a friend?) How can you create more of these?

THE RESET

Chapter 9: What Strength Actually Looks Like Now

For twenty-four years, my "strength" was an outward performance. It was loud, busy, and visually impressive. It looked like raising over $20,000 for NCCU while my own bank account of energy was overdrawn. It looked like working out every single day so a man who didn't deserve my heart would at least regret losing my body.

But I've learned that strength isn't always a heavy lift. Sometimes, strength is the courage to be "weak."

We have been taught that strength means pushing through, wearing the "Delivery Leader" armor, and never letting anyone see the cracks. We sit in the deafening silence of our empty houses, wearing a mask of "I'm fine," while drowning in a dark room with no doors. We feel ashamed that we can't just "bounce back" like a brand-new ball.

In this reset, I had to learn a different kind of power. Strength became the moment I stopped pretending. It was the text to my sister, or mom that said, "I'm not okay today." It was the decision to stay in bed and let the "Strong Friend" cape stay in the closet.

Strength is choosing to actually heal instead of just looking like you've healed.

The first time I practiced this new kind of strength, I wasn't expecting it.

May 9, 2025. My eyes were swollen from tears that refused to stop after I arrived back in Charlotte from Texas. I had just watched my son graduate from basic military training. I was so proud of his accomplishments, but I was also battling the unknown of when I'd see him again.

As I laid on my partner's shoulder at the airport, he held me and reassured me I'd be okay, that he'd be with me during this transition. I carried that hope with me as we traveled home.

After we got to long term parking, loaded our luggage in the car, and started the 20-minute drive home, everything changed.

What should have been a quiet ride of reflection, of celebrating a bittersweet but happy moment, turned into a whirlwind of profanity and hurled screams that left me shaken and frightened.

In a panic, I tried to call my mom to be a voice of reason. But my partner wanted the argument to stay isolated inside the moving luxury vehicle as we traveled down the road to the home we'd been sharing since August 2021.

After pleading without success for us to surrender to silence for the rest of the ride, I knew I had to create space for the safety of both of us. I pulled over at a local establishment and asked him to exit the vehicle.

He refused.

I waved for help. He got out.

I rushed home, pulled my car into the garage, and disabled the automated door. My hands were shaking, but my mind was clear. I moved his luggage from one vehicle to another. I grabbed his tools and work clothes and quickly placed them in his work truck. Time was on my side, and I knew the anger would turn into something worse if I didn't diffuse the moment.

Was it the right decision? I'll never know. But at that moment, it felt necessary. I had given him everything he needed for the next few days so calmer heads could prevail.

After he couldn't gain entry to the home, after my request for us to cool off for a day or two, he decided not to return. We began our journey living in two separate spaces.

Since March 24, 2025, one week after my son left for basic training and after six weeks of his new job having him travel across the country, he'd been staying with family or friends. He only came back to the area a few days out of the month.

What I thought would be a new adventure, a fun phase of being in a relationship with my fiancé without the responsibilities of being an everyday mom, turned out to be the beginning of my official empty nesting phase.

There I was, 45 years old. All my children were moving on to the next stage of their lives. And I sat quietly, questioning what would happen next.

Going into that weekend, a few days before May 11th, Mother's Day and my son's 20th birthday, I was alone, unsure of my decisions, still trying to figure out what happened on that short ride from the airport.

But a quiet voice inside my head knew it was the right decision to no longer live together.

My heart felt lighter. I knew the financial burden would catch up with me eventually, but peace in that moment was a strength I needed and embraced.

Gradually, once the initial shock faded, I took in my surroundings and understood that the resilience which helped me manage everything on my own from March 24th to May 9th would now have to support me through a lasting shift. I saw this change as a sign that our relationship was ending.

I also had to admit when I wasn't okay.

My 46th birthday was approaching May 31st, and I was in a place of total uncertainty. My relationship was in limbo. My son was across the country in training school. My daughter was setting up appointments for us to look at wedding dresses.

I was in a daze. Brain fog was an understatement.

I put on a brave face, but inside I was dealing with cracks in the foundation that would soon crumble if not addressed. I remember telling my mom that I was experiencing some heavy thoughts. It felt like a frog in my throat, a shakiness in my spirit that felt uneasy.

That was the moment I started to understand: Real strength isn't about how many rooms you can show up in. It's about knowing when to stay home and heal.

You don't have to prove anything to the CEO who let you go, the partner who moved out, or the children who are now flying on their own. The most unforgettable strength you can own is the honesty it takes to say, "I am recalibrating, and I am worth the wait."

Chapter 10: Who You're Becoming (Not Who You Were)

This pivot season is not an interruption of your life; it is the construction of your real one.

Even if you didn't choose this, even if you'd rather be back in 2019 before the world stopped, or back in the comfort of a predictable W2, this season is changing your DNA. It is refining what you tolerate and who you choose to keep close.

I used to miss the version of me that had a "plan." I missed the woman who walked across the NCCU stage in 2001, the one who knew how to grind through anything. But that version of me was built on survival. This version is being built on evolution.

Becoming happens in the quiet. It happened to me when I stopped being the "Everyday Manager" for my children and started becoming their Wise Counsel. It happened when I stopped investing 100% of my genius into "their" company and started believing that Stronger Than Before Creative Services wasn't just a side hustle, it was my destiny.

You aren't starting over from zero. You are starting from experience. Pay attention to the woman who is rising out of the rubble of October 2025. She is sharper, she is quieter, and she is no longer for sale.

The Values That Matter Now

When your world shifts, your compass has to be recalibrated.

A year ago, I valued the "magazine cover" life. I valued being part of a tall, athletic power couple. I valued the "Mrs." title I was planning for. But after the eggshells were swept away and the wedding plans were shredded, my values shifted.

I realized that peace is a higher currency than prestige.

At 25, I was in full mommy and wife mode. My daughter was only a toddler, and my belly was full of life to come. Graduate school was keeping me busy, along with so many things I had waited to achieve. I valued being needed, seen as capable, and proving that despite having a child at 15, I could still build something beautiful.

By 35, I was divorced. I had settled back in North Carolina after a pivot season that moved me from Southern California back home. I had endured things I don't talk about often, but I came out of it knowing exactly what I valued: boundaries, peace, and clarity.

My faith was strong. My boundaries were in place. I was going for what I wanted in the next phase of my life, and I wasn't apologizing for it.

Now, at 46, standing in the wreckage of everything I'd built, I value something even simpler: being at peace when I wake up.

That shift changed everything.

I started asking myself a new question before every decision: "Will this cost me my peace?" If the answer was yes, the answer was no.

Since being on eggshells, the last year of my long-term relationship, I now value boundaries, peace, and living my life unapologetically.

I decided to no longer do websites for clients. I removed a few other services to allow myself to rebrand Stronger Than Before Creative Services. I was able to gain an international client through collaboration, and I felt alignment starting to develop in the quiet moments.

Peace, for me, looks like this:

My morning workout routine. Those 30 to 45 minutes where it's just me, my body, and my breath.

Morning walks with my TikTok friends over FaceTime. We don't even have to talk the whole time. Just knowing someone else is moving with me makes the day feel lighter.

My teatime with my weekly book reading goals. I curl up in my favorite purple chair with chamomile tea and get lost in someone else's story for a while.

Daily check-ins on FaceTime with the people who matter. Not performative conversations, real ones.

Peace also means saying no without guilt.

In this season, I've learned to ask myself: What is the cost of my "Yes"?

If a relationship, a job, or a friendship costs me my sleep or forces me to adjust my anxiety meds, the price is too high.

I had to set a boundary with the world. I had to learn that having a routine, even if it's just me and silence, is more important than being "desired" by someone who doesn't see my soul.

Let your values be your anchor. When you know that your peace is non-negotiable, you stop moving out of fear of being alone and start moving with the intention of being whole.

Chapter 11: Rebuilding Confidence, One Small Promise at a Time

Confidence takes a massive hit when the things you "delivered" are no longer asked.

After that 3:15 PM call on October 31st, I didn't feel like the giant in the room anymore. I felt small. I felt overlooked. I felt like a line item that had been cut. When you lose your job and the partner in the same season, you start replaying every decision like a bad movie, wondering where you missed the cue.

But confidence after a pivot is not built by thinking harder; it's built by trusting the process.

Confidence came back in unexpected moments.

It wasn't when I landed a new client or got a compliment on my appearance. It came back through the small, daily promises I kept to myself.

The small daily promises looked simpler than I expected:

I got out of bed every day. I never slept in, even when my body begged me to stay under the covers. Getting vertical felt like a victory some mornings.

I tried to get some air if it wasn't raining. Even if it was just standing on the porch for five minutes, I needed to feel the sun on my face.

I waited at least 30 minutes in the morning before opening social media. I didn't need the world's noise in my head before I'd even had my tea. I needed to hear my own thoughts first.

I promised I would give God thanks and be grateful for what I do have. Even on the hard days, I'd whisper, "Thank you for breath. Thank you for shelter. Thank you for one more day to figure this out."

Working from home could have been an excuse to stay in pajamas all day, but I didn't let it. Daily, I would get dressed, put on light makeup, and present myself as I would for the office, not in a suit, but intentionally. It was a small act of self-respect.

I treated my "office days" seriously. When I "logged in" to work on my business, I treated it like W2. I gave it 10 to 12 hours if that's what was needed. I showed up for myself the way I used to show up for a company that didn't value me.

I took 15 to 30 minutes walking the cul-de- sacs to get off screen time. I'd check in with my mom, my homegirls, my sister, or my partner, whoever was available to chat during that time.

I started reading self-improvement books. Not to "fix" myself, but to remind myself that growth is still possible even in the rubble.

These weren't the promises of a high achiever. These were the promises of someone learning to be gentle with herself. But they were the foundation.

That morning, I published a LinkedIn post about the scholarship campaign without overthinking each word.

It was a phone call with a potential client where I named my rate without flinching, because my expertise was still valuable, title or no title.

It was the moment I looked in the mirror and started speaking kindly to the woman staring back, instead of mourning the one who used to be there.

Confidence after a fall doesn't announce itself with trumpets. It arrives quietly, in the moments when you realize you're no longer apologizing for taking up space.

I told myself I would breathe. I stopped the "revenge workouts" and started "recovery movements." I started treating my body like a home I planned to live in for a long time, not a battlefield.

You are still capable. You didn't lose your talent when you lost your title. You didn't lose your beauty when you lost your partner. You just lost the distractions.

Chapter 12: Keep It Simple

The "Delivery Leader" in me wanted to fix everything by Monday.

I wanted to have a new business plan, the healed heart, the perfect body, and the "Mrs." title all sorted out at once. That pressure is a lie. It takes you away from the only place where healing actually happens: Right here.

Don't make your reset a project to be managed. You don't need a 90-day roadmap. You just need to find stability in this twenty-four-hour block. Make your days simple so your spirit can finally catch its breath.

Progress in a reset looks different than progress in a corporation.

Progress is a morning where you don't feel the "weight" on your chest.

Progress is a night where you don't stay up through the 6-hour time difference just to prove you're "present."

Progress is choosing peace over urgency.

Take the next right step. If that step is just making a cup of tea and sitting in the sun, count it as a win. The big picture will paint itself when the canvas is dry.

Chapter 13: You Don't Have to Do This Alone

You were never meant to carry the weight of a collapsed world on your own shoulders.

I know the temptation to isolate. I know how easy it is to retreat into that dark room where there are no doors and the silence is so heavy it feels physical. For most of my life, I was the one people called. I was the rock. I was the person who stayed in control because I believed that if I let go, everyone else would fall apart. But I had to learn the hard way that there is a massive difference between being independent and being isolated. One is a choice; the other is a cage.

Support during a reset does not look like a crowd. It looks like the quiet, consistent presence of a few people who do not need you to be the Delivery Leader.

For me, support had to become intentional. It looked like therapy, where I finally had a safe space to say aloud that I was exhausted, angry, and felt discarded. It was the one place where I didn't have to provide structure or a strategic roadmap. I could just be Tashia.

Support also came through my faith, which shifted from a public performance to a private lifeline. It was about sitting in the still moments and trusting that even when I felt unsure and overlooked, I was still being guided by something higher than my own understanding.

And then there was the new connection.

Meeting someone while my world was falling apart felt both terrifying and necessary. I didn't go looking for it. In fact, I actively resisted it at first. I thought I needed to be "whole" before I could let anyone in. I thought I needed to have it all figured out.

But this connection taught me something I hadn't learned in eight years with my ex: Support doesn't mean fixing.

In my earlier relationship, I had learned to shrink. I learned to take the blame to avoid conflict. I learned to adjust my needs to match his comfort. I spent years walking on eggshells, convincing myself that was what love needed.

But with this new person, this man I had met during the campaign who lived across an ocean, I was learning a "different" language. He didn't need me to be the "Delivery Leader." He didn't need me to manage his emotions or carry the weight of the relationship on my shoulders. He just wanted to know me.

We built our connection slowly, across time zones and video calls. In December 2025, I traveled to Africa to meet him in person. That trip wasn't just about romance; it was about choosing to invest in the possibility instead of staying trapped in the past. It was about proving to myself that I was still a woman worth knowing, even without the job title, the ring, or the perfect family photo.

But I had to be honest with myself: Even in this beautiful new space,

I was still performing. I was staying awake through the six-hour time difference, determined not to repeat the mistakes of my last relationship. I wanted to be the "Perfect Partner" so badly that I was sacrificing the very "Pause" I was supposed to be giving myself.

True support only works when you stop performing. It took me months to realize that being loved didn't require me to be "on" 24/7. It meant letting someone see the hollow eyes behind the fit body. It meant admitting when I was tired, when I was overwhelmed, when I didn't have it all together.

You don't need everyone to understand your journey. You just need a few safe places where your soul can catch its breath. Letting yourself accept care is not a sign of weakness. It's the wisdom to realize that you deserve to be poured into, not just used as a source.

Let support be the foundation of your reset. It is the only way to ensure that when you stand back up, you are doing it from a place of wholeness instead of total exhaustion.

Reflection & Realignment

The reset will encourage you to look at strength differently, reconnect with your values, simplify your reset, and think about the support you need.

Before you move forward, take a moment to notice what's starting to settle into place.

You do not need to answer all of these all at once. These questions are not meant to rush you ahead but to help you stand more firmly where you are.

This is what realignment looks like. From here, you will be ready to begin again with intention.

Reflection:

1. Think real life: What does strength look like for you in this season?

2. What values are non-negotiable?

3. Where have you been pushing yourself when you needed to keep things simple?

4. Even if it's something small, what helps you rebuild trust in yourself?

5. What kind of support would make this reset feel more lasting?

Dig Deeper (Optional Journaling):

1. **Before & After Values:** Create two columns. In the first column, list what you valued a year ago (titles, appearances, being needed, etc.). In the second column, list what you value now. What changed? Why?

2. **The Cost of Yes:** Think of the last three times you said "yes" to something (a request, an event, a relationship demand). Did any of those "yeses" cost you your peace? What would have happened if you'd said no?

3. **Confidence Inventory:** List 5 things you're still good at,
    even without the job title, the relationship, or the old roles.
    (Examples: You're a good listener. You can organize
    anything. You tell the truth. You show up for people. You
    survive hard things.)

4. **Support Audit:** Who has actually shown up for you during
    this pivot? (Not who you expected to show up, who actually
    did.) How can you let them know they matter?

5. **Future Values:** Imagine yourself one year from now, living aligned with your values. What does a typical Tuesday look like? What are you saying no to? What are you protecting?

THE RESTART

Chapter 14: You're Not Starting from Zero

Let's be honest. Starting again is humbling. It can feel like a step backward when you realize your unemployment is ending, there's no W2 in sight, and the career you spent decades building feels like a closed book. You might have thought you'd be more settled by now, more certain of your next move. Realizing you're standing in the middle of a "zero" moment brings up a mix of fear and frustration.

But you have to realize that starting again is not starting from nothing.

You are starting with twenty years of being a present mother. You are starting with the leadership skills that raised over $20,000 for NCCU students while your own tank was empty. You are starting with the wisdom of a woman who knows exactly what it feels like to walk on eggshells and has decided she will never do it again.

I don't believe in defeat. Even as I navigate the uncertainty of this gap, I know that my past did not stop my purpose, it prepared it. You know what hurts, what you cannot accept anymore, and what you refuse to repeat. That awareness is your greatest asset.

Starting again isn't about proving your worth to a recruiter; it is about choosing to move forward with an intentional spirit instead of a fearful one. Nothing you have been through is wasted. Everything you have learned is coming with you into the next room.

Here's what I'm not starting from nothing with:

I know how to manage complex projects with tight deadlines, which came from being a Delivery Leader. Operational management. Roadmap and program management planning. Strategic alignment. Executive communication. Contract management. Delivery implementation. Problem solving and support. Presentation and public speaking.

These skills didn't disappear when the company let me go. They're mine. They always were.

I know how to fundraise and build community. I learned how to tell a story that moves people. I learned how to mobilize strangers into action. I learned that my voice has power, even when I don't feel powerful.

I know how to show up even when I don't feel ready, that came from twenty-five years of being a mother who didn't have the luxury of falling apart in front of her kids.

Being a mom means I didn't have the luxury of taking a day off unless it was a planned vacation, and even then, I was on duty at all times. I had to be the cook, the cleaner, the driver, the teacher, and more. I had to wear all the hats. Motherhood is a full-time job, and for 25 years, that's what I did.

I learned that love isn't supposed to shrink you, and I learned that by experiencing eight years of a relationship where I made myself small at times just to keep the peace.

That relationship taught me hard lessons that I'm now bringing into new connections:

Be more intentional. Take moments to show appreciation for the other person. Not because you have to perform, but because you genuinely see them.

Don't hold back. Give your all without restrictions. Leave the past hurts in the past and don't punish someone new for what someone old did.

Match energy. Be with someone who gives the same energy that matches yours. No more one-sided effort.

Be honest about how you feel. Treat the person like a friend first. Be mindful of how busy you can get but also be flexible.

Voice your perspective. It's okay to have a unique perspective and to voice it. You don't have to make yourself small to save someone else's feelings.

Recognize the lesson. People come into your life to teach you a lesson or to help you through a lesson. Recognizing the lesson early on will help shape the next journey.

I know my voice has power, which came from every presentation,

every campaign, every moment I stood in a room and delivered
results.

**This isn't starting over. This is taking everything you have
mastered and finally applying it to something that belongs to
you.**

Chapter 15: The Lessons You're Taking With You

Every season of silence has taught me something that noise would have drowned out.

This season taught me that God sometimes uses separation to create the space needed for a new story to be written. I had to be separated from the busy schedule of everyday motherhood. I had to be separated from a job structure that did not value my soul. I even had to be separated from a long-term relationship that no longer fit the woman I was becoming.

I have realized that growth is not always a loud breakthrough. Sometimes growth is the quiet recognition that I have outgrown what I once prayed for. That realization does not come with fireworks. It comes with stillness. It comes with uncomfortable clarity.

And in that stillness, support showed up in ways I never expected.

While some people I assumed would remain close slowly disappeared, strangers stepped forward. An entire TikTok community showed up in ways I never expected. What started as a platform for teaching and connection quietly became a lifeline.

It was mid-May 2025 when I began connecting more intentionally with a group of women on TikTok. At first, it was casual conversation. We talked about life, families, work, and random moments of the day. Slowly, those conversations deepened.

One woman in particular began walking daily during the summer. She was a teacher and had the summer off. She invited others to join her virtually. I started waking up early to walk with her before my first meeting of the day.

Those walks did more for my spirit than she probably realized.

Some mornings we talked about nothing serious. Other mornings we laughed. Some mornings were full of shopping, breathing, and simply moving our bodies. But in that season, when it was hard for me to hold my head up emotionally, those walks grounded me.

She poured into others even when her own well was not full. Watching her show up consistently helped me find consistency in myself.

When school started back, the daily walks ended. I missed them more than I expected. But the connection did not disappear. We still check in. We still speak encouragement. We still show up for one another online in small but meaningful ways.

I met women from different states, different countries, and diverse backgrounds. Two of them I speak to daily. They are like sisters I did not grow up with but somehow needed in this season of my life.

Meeting new people at this stage of life stretched me. It reminded me not to put God in a box. Support does not always come from where I expect it. Sometimes it comes from across the world. Sometimes it comes from someone who only knows me as "Pretty Queen."

When I posted about the NCCU scholarship campaign, I expected modest engagement. Maybe a few shares and a couple of donations.

Instead, the campaign caught momentum.

Hundreds of people, most of whom had never met me, shared it, donated, and left comments filled with encouragement.

One woman said on a livestream I was hosting, "You're pouring into students while you're barely holding yourself together. That's not a weakness. That's strength."

I cried when I heard that.

She saw what I could not see yet.

My pain was not stopping my purpose. It was shaping it.

In looking for support to amplify that campaign, I connected with an entertainer and promoter whose company, MDE Empire Promotions, helped push the message further than I could have done alone. What began as a professional collaboration slowly became personal, and that transition taught me something I did not know I still needed to learn.

At the same time, my Alpha Kappa Alpha sisters showed up in ways that reminded me I was never meant to carry life alone.

During this season, I took part in a Secret Soror exchange. Each month, we sent thoughtful gifts to another soror based on a survey. We did not know who our Secret Soror was until the end of the year.

The soror assigned to me consistently sent warm, intentional gifts and notes. During months when I felt especially low, her encouragement felt like oxygen.

For my birthday, she sent cozy socks, an inspirational mug, a soft blanket, and other small gifts she knew I would love. That birthday was my first as an empty nester. My earlier relationship was in limbo, and my emotions were layered and complicated. I curled up in my favorite purple chair, wrapped in that blanket, sipping chamomile tea, and allowed myself to just be.

It was bittersweet.

At that moment, I felt seen. I felt loved. I felt like I mattered, even when parts of me felt invisible.

Sisterhood is not about public appearances. It is about being a net when someone is falling.

And then there is the new relationship.

For almost eight years, I equated intensity with passion. I believed that conflict meant depth. I thought love required sacrifice in ways that slowly erased parts of me.

This new connection is teaching me something quieter.

Love does not have to be loud to be real, although he will proudly shout his love from Africa to America without hesitation. What I am learning is that love can be steady. It can be safe. It can allow space.

I do not have to perform to be valued. I do not have to shrink to keep peace. Energy matters. Presence matters. Being seen matters.

Healthy love does not demand constant proving. It does not weaponize silence. It does not require me to earn rest.

It simply allows me to be.

And that lesson may be one of the most important ones I carry forward.

This season did not just remove things from my life. It clarified what belongs. It showed me who shows up. It revealed what I will no longer tolerate. It reminded me that purpose continues, even when circumstances shift.

What leaves your life makes room for what can finally see you.

The space may feel uncomfortable, but it is not empty. It is being rearranged for something that can meet you as you are now, not who you used to be.

Chapter 16: The Next Right Step

I do not need a massive 50-page business plan to move forward.

I just need the next right step.

For a long time, I kept Stronger Than Before Creative Services on the back burner. I convinced myself it could not sustain me, so I gave my best hours, my clearest thinking, and my strongest leadership to other people's companies. I built systems. I delivered results. I helped other people meet their goals.

And then I would be exhausted.

In this restart, I had to ask myself a hard question:

Why was I so willing to bet on everyone else, but hesitant to bet on myself?

That question sat with me for weeks.

The truth is, I was afraid. Afraid that if I gave my full energy to my own vision and it didn't work, I would have no one else to blame. A W2 gave me structure. It gave me validation. It gave me a title I could hide behind.

But it also kept me small.

In this season, I am applying that same discipline and structure to myself.

Living my brand daily does not look glamorous. It looks like consistency. It looks like waking up and doing my spiritual routine even when my mind is heavy. It looks like writing when no one is watching. It looks like showing up for Stronger Than Before the same way I once showed up for a corporation.

It also looks like trusting opportunities that do not pay at once.

Working alongside MDE Empire Promotions company in Lagos, Nigeria as a strategic operations partner has stretched me. It is not financially compensating yet, but it is expanding my reach, my network, and my belief in what is possible.

This partnership reminds me that not every win comes in the form of a paycheck. Some wins come as positioning, preparation, and alignment. I feel alignment matters.

There are days when doubt still whispers. Days when I wonder if I should just "play it safe." Days when I feel the weight of responsibility more heavily than confidence.

But persistence does not require perfect confidence.

Persistence looks like keeping my word to myself.

It looks like staying intentional in small decisions.

It looks like holding onto Jeremiah 29:11 when my timeline feels uncertain.

It looks like refusing to downplay my God-given talent.

I am not waiting to feel fearless.

I am moving while feeling human.

The only way forward is forward, even if the steps are quiet.

You do not need the whole blueprint. You only need the courage to take the next right step.

Chapter 17: Words to Carry You Forward

Words have power, especially when your thoughts are trying to convince you that you've lost yours. I started each morning in late 2025 with three affirmations from **Norman Vincent Peale**. These became my lifeline when I couldn't find my own voice:

I expect the best and with God's help I will obtain the best.

The rough is only mental. I think victory, I get victory.

I do not believe in defeat.

But I also needed affirmations that spoke directly to my specific season, the empty nest, the ended engagement, the job loss, the new beginning. So, I created these.

Use them. Adapt them. Write your own. Just don't skip this practice. On the days when your thoughts are heavy, let these words carry you.

For the Empty Nester:

My children's independence is not my irrelevance. I raised them to fly.

I am still a mother, even when they don't need me daily.

The quiet house is not empty; it's finally making room for me.

I did my job well, and now I get to discover who I am beyond "Mom."

For the Job Loss / Career Pivot:

I was not discarded; I was redirected.

My value is not tied to a title, a paycheck, or someone else's org chart.

I am the CEO of my own life, and my business is worth building.

What's meant for me will not require me to beg for it.

I am a strategist, a visionary, and a survivor.

The skills I built in 20 plus years didn't disappear, they're mine, and I'm taking them with me.

For the Ended Relationship:

I am allowed to grieve what ended, even if it needed to end.

Peace is a higher currency than being wanted by someone who made me small.

I am not too old, too difficult, or too much. I am exactly enough.

The right person will not require me to perform or shrink.

I deserve love that feels like rest, not a performance review.

For Identity Rebuilding:

I am not starting over; I am starting from experience.

Who I am is not defined by who needs me.

I am a woman still becoming, and that is enough.

My purpose is still unfolding, even as my roles change.

For Faith in the Pivot:

I trust that even when I feel alone, I am being held.

God doesn't need my performance; He wants my presence.

This season is not punishment; it's preparation.

The Lord is close to the brokenhearted. That includes me.

I will say "Yes, Lord" even when I don't understand the plan.

For Moving Forward:

I choose faith over fear, every single hour.

Small steps are still steps. Progress is not a sprint.

I trust myself to make wise choices, even when I feel unsure.

This is not the end of my story; it's the beginning of my reset.

I am stronger than before because I survived what tried to break me.

Journal Your Way Through

If you've made it this far in the book, you've done the challenging work of pausing, feeling, and acknowledging. You've given yourself permission to be human in the middle of a pivot. Now it's time to go deeper, not because you have to, but because you're ready.

These journaling prompts aren't homework. They're invitations. Some will make you cry. Some will make you angry. Some will make you realize you've been carrying things that were never yours to hold. Take your time with them. There's no deadline.

Prompts:

1. **What version of yourself are you grieving right now?**
   (The title? The relationship? The daily routine? The future you thought you'd have?)

2. **If your pivot is a rescue mission, what is it rescuing you from?** (Be honest. Even if it hurts.)

3. **What would you do differently if you knew no one was watching or judging?**

4. **Who do you become when you're not performing?** (Take off the cape. Who's underneath?)

5. **What does peace feel like in your body?** (Not what you think it should feel like, what it actually feels like for you.)

6. **Write a letter to the person who hurt you (your ex, your former boss, yourself).** You don't have to send it. Just write it.

7. **If your 60-year-old self could talk to you right now, what would she say?**

8. **What are you carrying that doesn't belong to you anymore?** (Shame? Blame? Someone else's expectations?)

9. **What small promise can you keep today?**

Chapter 18: You're Ready

This is not the end of your story. It is the turning point. It is the moment you stopped being the passenger in your own life and decided to take the wheel again.

You paused. You grieved. You faced the silence instead of running from it. You allowed yourself to feel what most people try to numb or push away. That is strength. Not the loud kind. Not the kind that smiles while quietly falling apart. Real strength.

When life forced you to pivot, you could have rushed to replace what was lost. You could have filled the space with noise, distractions, or quick decisions just to prove that you were fine. Instead, you chose to steady yourself. You let the shock settle. You acknowledged the grief. You sat with the tough questions about identity and worth. You focused on rebuilding your footing before trying to rebuild your life.

That matters more than you think.

I even traveled across the world to Africa to strengthen connections that are grounding me now. Not because I had every answer and not because everything felt secure, but because I was no longer willing to let fear make my decisions. This pivot showed me something powerful. Growth does not wait for clarity. Sometimes clarity follows movement.

Starting again does not need certainty. It requires courage. It requires honesty. It requires faith when your confidence feels thin. It requires taking one step even when you cannot see the entire staircase.

You are not behind. You are not broken. You are becoming. And becoming is not rushed. It is formed over time, shaped by what you have survived and strengthened by what you have learned.

As you move forward, you may notice a new question rising quietly within you. Who am I now, and how do I rebuild my life in a way that fits this season?

That question is not pressure. It is an invitation.

When Life Forces You to Pivot was about stabilizing your footing. It was about giving yourself permission to pause instead of pretending. It was about honoring your grief instead of performing strength. It was about resetting before rebuilding.

The next phase is coming. In the next book, The Reset Season: Rebuilding After a Career or Life Disruption, coming soon, we will move into reconstruction. We will talk about rebuilding your identity when old roles no longer fit. We will talk about creating routines that honor your energy and redefining success on your own terms. We will talk about designing a life that reflects who you are now, not who you used to be.

But for now, just breathe.
You have come further than you realize. You have survived what tried to dismantle you. You have found steadiness in a season that once felt unstable.

Be patient with yourself. Do not rush the person you are becoming.

This is not the end of your story. It is the beginning of your reset.

You survived the pivot. Now watch what you build from it.

About the Author

Tashia R. Jones is a strategist, a visionary, and a woman who understands what it means to rebuild when life shifts without warning.

After navigating an empty nest, the end of a long-term relationship, and a sudden career disruption within the same season, she found herself standing at a crossroads she did not choose but had to face.

Instead of collapsing under the weight of the silence, she leaned into faith, honest reflection, and the wisdom of her own lived experience. What began as personal survival slowly became a calling to help others navigate their own quiet battles.

A proud graduate of North Carolina Central University and a member of Alpha Kappa Alpha Sorority, Incorporated, Tashia has spent years being a strong friend and the steady leader for others. Through her reset season, she learned that strength is not only about delivering for everyone else. It is also about healing yourself with the same excellence and care.

She is the Founder and Principle Consultant of **Stronger Than Before Creative Services**, a brand she has owned since 2008 and is now living more fully than ever before.

When Life Forces You to Pivot is the first book in a three-part journey "The Reset Trilogy" series created to help readers pause, realign, and rebuild with clarity and confidence.

Tashia believes that a pivot is not an ending. It is an invitation to become more grounded, more aware, and more aligned than before.

Connect with Tashia:
Stronger Than Before Creative Services
www.strongerthanb4.org